Foreword:

"By the Candlelig̶l̶ [barcode] ᵧ ᵾᵾᵾᵧ woman's descent into the darkness of her subconscious. For the reader, the experience is designed to feel like an elevator going all the way to the ground floor. This book of poetry is best enjoyed in the dark, in the quiet, in the music, in bed, and by the candlelight — or just the light from your smartphone if that's all you have.

Dedication:

To every version of myself in every lifetime at every age. May you be vindicated.

Playlist:

Spring

1.Nighttime thoughts

When the desire within you to change is
stronger than the desire to stay the same
No wonder you can't sleep
There's a battle going on in your head
Fists are clenched
Pupils are dilated
Eyebrows are furrowed
And there is a rage between the three of
you
Who you were, who you are, and who
you're going to be

2. C. A. L. M.

C is for cool hands all over my body
Running across my temple
Tickling my back
Fingering my hair
Some nice, loving spirit with their hands all
over me.

A is for autumn leaves on grandma's front
porch
Watching them dance in the wind like it's
their opening night
Pirouettes, arabesques, grand jétés
All in the heat of the night

Laying themselves open to my view

L is for light
I'm sleeping on air in a cold, damp room
with no blankets
Feeling like a feather
Or I'm playing peek-a-boo with the sun
Through the leaves
And I catch a glimpse of myself in a mirror
With a reflection off of my eyes showing that
pretty, drowning, milky brown color I was
given

M is for mystery
The darkness
Things I can't see and a cool night's breeze
Deep and dark like the middle of the ocean
I'm falling deeper and slower
Asleep in the water's cold, wet grasp
I can't see
And I don't need to

3. Big.

My hands are tied and I'm chained to the
floor.

That floor is the foundation of the room.

That room is in the right hand corner of the
lowest level.

The lowest level has five other levels stacked on top of it.

Those levels are pieced together into the shape of a boat.

That boat is in the middle of the ocean.

That ocean is in the middle of the world.

The world is in the middle of the Galaxy.

The Galaxy is in the middle of the universe.

The universe is in the palm of God's hands.

I am small and trapped and strong and avenged.

4. To My First

To say that I love would be an understatement.

To say that I love would be unnecessary.

To say that I love would be pathetic.

To say that I love would be ignored.

To say that I love would be unbelievable.

To say that I love would be unfathomable.

To say that I love would be humbling.

To say that I love would be personal.

To say that I love would be painful.

To say that I love would be honest.

To say that I love would be vulnerable.

To say goodbye

Has been beautiful.

5. Real Talk

Say something real

Anything real

Tonight is not the night for I'm beautiful or
you love me

Something non-generic, please

Pick my brain

I want to hold a person not an idea

Give me sweet reminders of who you are

Answers all wrapped up inside you

Pressed tightly together

Like the inside of a kiss

Don't lie to me

Just tell me something real

6. Butterflies in Threes

I let myself fall into a sea of strange
butterflies

They fly past me in groups of three

Twisting on each other's vibrations

Like gravity they pull me as close to the
center as possible

I prefer to walk around the edges avoiding
contact

7. Boogieman

Somewhere far away from myself

I found you

Strange, half erect creature standing in the
hallway

You opened your mouth and all my dirty
laundry fell out

Every nightmare, every bad thought

Pushed me closer to the edge of my bed

I covered my eyes and felt you stare harder

Cloaked in darkness with my sanity
clenched in your palm

I am left all alone with Him

I can't breathe

I'm too far away from my lungs

No heartbeat

I'm too far away from my energy

No vision

I'm too far away from my eyes

In a bed

In a room

Somewhere far away from myself

Summer

8. In Love & Light

Wrapped in white and red

I am at home in the moonlight

Dust and Mist fill me up and cover me from head to toe

As I hang from the crescent's feet

I fear nothing in the darkness

Yet at daybreak I run

Drawn towards the noontime rays as fast as my hips can carry me

Short bursts of heat fall on my back

On my arms

On my legs

Slowly overwhelming me until I become the light

I become the sun

And as my sun sets I slow to a walk

Embracing the cool, damp night air as it washes over me

Then I sigh and part ways with the day

As the moon pulls me under completely

And I land gently among the stars

9. When You Can't Get Out of Bed

You're going to roll over

You're going to wake up

And instantly the pain will shake hands with your consciousness

You're starting over from scratch

But you get quicker and more efficient at piecing yourself back together everyday

Every 24 hours

You convince yourself to be in love with
what you see in the mirror

Yesterday you found yourself singing

The day before you found yourself on the
bus

The day before that you found yourself in
the shower

You are not your bad thoughts

You are not your sad thoughts

You are not weak enough to be washed
away in your pain

You found yourself the day before

The day before

And the day before

And you will find yourself today

at your own pace

You want to be okay

And you can be

You'll be okay everyday

Until one day

You'll roll over

You'll wake up

And the person greeting your
consciousness will be there with love

Love for 24 hours

You'll be okay

Everyday

So wake up

Roll over

And go find yourself.

10. For the Second

Change is measured in distance

Space

And time

A thousand miles is not as drastic

As across the country seems to be

And across the country is not as drastic as
three weeks and two time zones away

I separate myself from you in a cloudy haze

With distance

Space

And time

11. Cognitive Dissonance

It's a strange position to find yourself in

When you're doing the opposite of what's
going on in your head

And you can't stop

Cognitive dissonance takes on a new
meaning here in my body

I was dancing and screaming at the same
time

While you watched the ache in my hips rock
back and forth

You saw the crooked in my smile

Yet you did nothing to stop me

Press my heart and my body, back together

Outrace my mind

Outpace my lips

Ground me

12. Damn Promise

I've been trying to figure out why a man
makes his promise

Since I learned how to lie

It's a curious thing that we humans do

But we'll break our own hearts

On account of somebody else's promise

We'll forget how to write a happy tune

Or a love song about ourselves

Or a conversation that we had with God

On account of somebody else's promise

We lose ourselves in misplaced despair

and fall into depression

Instead of breathing in the good days past like oxygen

and exhaling all of the sad moments

Because of somebody else's promise

I was in a white room with white sheets and white pillowcases and white walls

The contrast of my black skin

Made it abundantly clear to me that my Black spirit did not belong

I had to move on account of my own promise

Not the lies my mama told

Not the lies my daddy told

Not brother

Not sister

Not boyfriend

Not girlfriend

I had to move

On my own damn promise.

13. A Time to..

I'm in a weird type of space

In this place there is time for everything

And everything has its time

There is a time to be in love

There is a time for sunshine

There is a time to be ugly

There is a time for passive resistance

There is a time for free

There is a time for me to do just as I please

When I please

However I please

I am in a space

That is mine

14. Fire Within

Some lives are meant to be more like shooting stars

And then others are like the sun

Real

Live

Hot souls on fire

I'm burning up

On top of this world

Alone without being lonely

Until I'm lonely

Because I am fire

Working my way from the inner volcanoes in my bones

To the earthquakes in between my toes

To the wildfires around my head

Shooting stars are passing me by

But in the night sky

I am still the sun.
The sun never stops shining

The earth just moves around her

15. *Vision Board*

I saw a vision

Of a brown woman

Coming to visit me in the night time

She walked with diamonds dangling from
her hips

She spoke with sugar on her lips

Her hands were soft and sweet up and
down my spine

She held me while I choked back tears

And with unwavering patience taught me
the names of the stars

With her arms wide and outstretched for me

Like I'm somebody to love

Like I'm somebody to see

I run wild under her protection

Like I'm somebody to lose

Touching every cloud

Getting real familiar with God

16. Power Leverage and Negotiation

I am always

Stuck

In the between place

Where things are as they are

And where things are as they should be

I move between

The powerful and powerless

To push things as close to perfection

As they can go

17. Strawberry Leaves

Brown legs

White teeth

Latching on to strawberry leaves

Feeling blue

Gray

Yellow

Feeling light

Feeling envied

Feeling whole

I chew on strawberry leaves

In the summertime

On my front porch

Picking fruit out of my mason jar

Sucking honey suckle

Tasting honey dews

Fingering grapes

All fruit

All fresh

All mine

In the sunlight

Chewing on strawberry leaves

Hoping it will

Make me just as sweet

18. Black southern belle

Humid summer nights are the price we pay

For the sweetest tea in the land

Front porch swings and my auntie's
lemonade

Bring me to peace

Walking lands that have known me all my
life

And being free in a way that mother's
mother's mother never was

I am compelled to rebellion and revolution

Being colored

And free

And southern

In a way that seems to conflict with the very fabric

That was used to weave this country together

Manufacturing biracial edges and white women blush

To prove that I am better at being you

And I can linger in and out of both spaces

The dream of a slave

Was the whisper of freedom's song through her

Unspoken womb

Fall

19. Fuck UNC.

I fell hard

Slowly and then all at once

Towards waves cracking beneath the weight
of my lower back

Towards screams echoing out through the
bottom of my lungs

Towards riot gear

Towards marching men

Towards guns and tasers and fear of a new
Black power and stature

We faced death

And no one on campus is talking about it

Man

Fuck the police and UNC.

20. Let it go, K.

There is a quiet peace in sudden dignity

Hope laced with resignation

The truth of the matter laid open

The sensitive underbelly anticipating the
strike from pain' s sharp edge

I am nothing

It means nothing

And for everything

There is nothing I can do

But be nothing

Nothing in everything that I am

Graceful descending of grace-filled descendants

Ancestors are whispering in my ear

"Now that is my girl."

21. Earth Below.

The truth is that I don't think I'm good enough

Remembering every intimate form of rejection from another individual

Validates my smallness

It's not that I don't know that everything is not for everyone

I am within and without consequence

The most important truth is that of liberation

The fault in my description of myself

Is that the sufficient clause is not necessary

I am not the center

But I am the circle

I am wholly and perfectly designed

So that I can facilitate love in the center

And say to myself and my daughter and my daughter's daughter

Powerful woman

You were once precious

You were once fragile

You were once shattered

But you have fallen

Gracefully

Unabashedly

And we will sink deep into the earth

Brown

Musky

Hot

Earth

Until we come up to breathe on the other
side of the world

Not as solid rock

But as cool Georgia mud

Powerful woman

I ground you.

22. *Disgusting.*

There was no part of me that he hadn't
touched

So how could I love myself now that he's
gone

Everything about me attracted him

Everything about me is the reason why I
hurt

Silently

Out Loud

Pain is pain is pain is earned

And I earned him

He's all over me like my own skin

Obsessing

Disgusting

You're disgusting

You're disgusting.

23. Crush.

I love you and I expect nothing in return.

I loved you and I expected nothing in return.

I will always love you and I expect nothing in return.

I love you

I expect nothing

I love

I expect

24. Chasadee is usually right.

The only way to get to freedom is through restraint

Restraining the parts that I decide I don't want

Playing God with the insides of my insides

This ain't surface level type of shit

Meanwhile

You're laughing out loud in a quiet body

After body after body after body

And you drag that laughter

That pain

That joy

That fear

That promise

Around with you

After body after body after body

Being God could never be easy

Playing God with human bodies

After body after body after body

Until you decide enough is enough

And stop deciding to be a part of the bodies

The quiet, laughing bodies

That never refrain from being quiet

And never refrain from laughing

I choose all at once to sing

Instead of laugh in silence

Restraining what would come naturally

Living with you

Watching you

Learning from you

Damn if my roommate isn't right about this shit.

25. Baggage.

If I had a bag for every time someone
diagnosed me with their own problem

Or contradicted their own truths

I might be able to set up shop

Someone said I had baggage and then
asked me to hold his shit.

Someone said I was crazy in the middle of a
nervous breakdown

Someone said I was too skinny while almost
starving themselves to death

Someone said my hair was too kinky and
asked if they could play in it

Someone said my politics was too racial
and then asked me why Black people act
like that

Someone said that my love was too Gay
and then kissed his own image in a mirror

Someone said my civil rights were
unattainable and then asked me to do my
civic duty

Someone said that I was childish and then
played games with my emotions

Someone said that I had baggage after handing me all of their bullshit.

26. Light.

When I opened the door

The reflection through the window at the end of the hall greeted me

10 feet ahead

Light sprawled out on the floor

She told me to move

I kept walking and the light grew bigger and bigger

Until I realized

That I am the light.

Winter

27. Shadows

You only need a slight modification in tone to discern whether one is looking at life and saying "Is that it?" with disdain for the past or disdain for the future. A shift in perspective. Revolutionary ramblings begging to be noticed. Begging to be more than mediocre. My writing is mediocre compared to the musings of my ancestors who could not read. My spirituality is child's play compared to the curse the witchdoctor's before me endured so that I could be here to heal. I used to be afraid of the dark but I am the dark. I am the shadow. I am the boogie monster. I am the god. I am the hero. I am the villain. Projections on a screen feel like different dimensions that are requesting my presence and all I wanted to do was rest. I thought that darkness meant I was evil now, but it just means that I am concealed. It just means that I am incalculable. It just means that I am beyond your capacity for understanding. And you don't even understand yourself.

You don't even understand the vibratory complexities of every well-intentioned smile and prayer.

Is your god a statue?

Is your god a book?

Is your god a memory?

Does your god rise sharply at 3 AM with tears in her eyes?

Does she light a candle when she prays?

Does she hold space for the bad things?

Does Satan know he's evil?
Does a moth know it's not a butterfly?

28. Darkness is Submersion
The longer I sit in darkness
The better I can see
Weeping willows in the distance
The building of self
Sculpting blind
Cycles of movement in my fingers
Crawling under my nails
And pulling the strings
Reminding me how your face looked in my head
Eyes like mine but stronger
Smile like mine but knowing

29. Tentative Love
Laugh lines peek out at me
Rough hands perform gently
Genuity in sensation
But the contrast from danger to safety still feels harsh
Like the rug on the floor of your heart
could be swept out from under you at any moment
The laugh lines disappear
And the contrast from safety to isolation feels familiar

30. Piston in the Caliber

The feeling I get when I'm the most aware of
my love for you
Is like a light turning on
Or the brake pads brushing against the rotor
The capacity is always there
Humming and flowing beneath the surface
Waiting to bring about a change in energy
Fate or God or Destiny fucks around with
the vibes
And when the energy does change
I allow my entire world to change too
even though I always see you coming

31. Million Miles

Changes in weather and
Deep sighs
Frowning face turning into laughing lines
I would drive a million miles to come home
to you

*32. "Oh, so you're into that Woo-Woo shit
now, huh?"*

The truth is in the cards
Is in your consciousness
Is in your intuition
Is in Spirit
Is in you
Popping out of the deck
Demanding clarity

33. Subconscious

You're running rampant through my
subconscious
Exercising control I never meant to give you
Vast grounds within the sea of my inner
thoughts
And you're the only solid thing I can see
clearly in my dreams
I feel guilty
Like I should turn away
Like you shouldn't be here
Like this late night rendez-vous is too
intimate
How did I get here?
How did you?

34. Used To

I used to write long lines
I used to be able to touch myself without
feeling ashamed
I used to believe in God
I used to dance
I used to eat every day
I used to pray
I used to sleep
I used to love easy
I used to trust people
I used to say what I feel
I used to like the color yellow

I used to wish I could swim in the ocean
I used to dream of being a princess
And those parts of me were used to control
me

35. Do I Miss You?

I've had a recurring thought
About my last moments in my past life
Someone crying
Someone loving
Someone worth staying for
Dreams as a little girl of him shouting my
name
Billions of people in the world and I'm
missing one
If I could remember your face, are you alive
for me to find you?
Are you right beside me and I don't know it?
Was I reincarnated here to elevate by
missing you?
Will I give birth to you in your next form?
This feeling of panic rising in my throat
Familiar
Is this yours?
Is this for you?
When I transitioned, did I leave something
behind?
Will you follow me?

36. Black Pussy Living

A purging.
A cleansing.
An echo.
A cycle.
Longing to close the closet door and not be
afraid of the shadow.
to love Her
to love the Journey.
to not be able to love the Journey more if I
named my daughter after Her.
Sacred space in my womb
Will one day be a hall of history books
What will I have them write about me?
About my pussy?
About my heart?
About the secrets my daughter will never
see?
About my husband cheating?
About stabbing my way through a bar full of
men?
About killing my baby?
About being a whore?
About living.
Black. Pussy. Living.
She whispers.
She is alive in you.
Shut up and let her speak.

37. *[untitled]*

I think it's kinda telling that
I only learned how to forgive everyone else

After realizing that I was already acquainted
with what was unforgivable.
I think it's kinda telling that I hadn't known
love
Until I knew the unlovable.

38. The Moment.

God
Please let this be the moment that I take
control.
Please let this be the moment that I stand
on my own two feet.
Please let this be the moment that I assert
myself.
Please let this be the moment that I tell
everyone else to fuck off.
Please let this be the moment where I get
comfortable being alone.
Where I accept that I crave solitude.
Please let this be the moment where I
accept responsibility.
Please let this be the moment where I resist
the urge to run away.
Please let this be the moment where I stop
living between adolescence and adulthood.
The expectations, the constructs.
Fuck it.Take me to the moment where I run
out of fucks to give

39. Unlock The Damn Door.

Unlock the damn door
Uncross me
Un-jinx me
Un-hex me
Un-white me
Un-curse me
Un-colonize me
Un-capitalize me
Un-hustle me
Un-fuck me
Un-fetishize me
Let me shed all of these make-believe
concepts that no longer apply
Unlock the damn door
Open the road, please sir

Made in the USA
Columbia, SC
25 March 2024

33264742R10022